LESLIE CAPLAN

Tales of Goha

Stories based on 'Myths and Legends of the Swahili'
by Dr Jan Knappert

HEINEMANN

INTERMEDIATE LEVEL

Series Editor: John Milne

The Heinemann Guided Readers provide a choice of enjoyable reading material for learners of English. The series is published at five levels – Starter, Beginner, Elementary, Intermediate and Upper. At **Intermediate Level**, the control of content and language has the following main features:

Information Control

Information which is vital to the understanding of the story is presented in an easily assimilated manner and is repeated when necessary. Difficult allusion and metaphor are avoided and cultural backgrounds are made explicit.

Structure Control

Most of the structures used in the Readers will be familiar to students who have completed an elementary course of English. Other grammatical features may occur, but their use is made clear through context and reinforcement. This ensures that the reading, as well as being enjoyable, provides a continual learning situation for the students. Sentences are limited in most cases to a maximum of three clauses and within sentences there is a balanced use of adverbial and adjectival phrases. Great care is taken with pronoun reference.

Vocabulary Control

There is a basic vocabulary of approximately 1,600 words. Help is given to the students in the form of illustrations, which are closely related to the text.

Glossary

Some difficult words and phrases in this book are important for understanding the story. Some of these words are explained in the story, some are shown in the pictures, and others are marked with a number like this . . .[3] Words with a number are explained in the Glossary on page 61.

Contents

A Note About These Stories

One thousand years ago, Baghdad was one of the most important cities in the world. It was the capital of a great empire. The city of Baghdad was ruled by a famous Caliph and a Caliph was like a prince. The Caliph was the most powerful man in the city and he could do anything he liked.

Because this Caliph was a wise man, he had many people who visited him in his palace. They were wise people who came to advise him.

The Caliph's palace was called the court. And at court he had doctors, lawyers and bankers to give him advice. In fact he had every kind of person in his court that he needed in order to rule Baghdad well. The richest, the most powerful, and the cleverest people, all met at the court.

Goha was the most famous of all the people in the court at that time. He was the court poet and he was also the court jester. A jester is a person who says and does things which make people laugh. The things a jester does are called tricks. Goha played many tricks on the other advisors and also on the Caliph himself. His tricks were always funny. For this reason the Caliph was always ready to forgive Goha and to laugh at his jokes.

The stories that follow are stories that were told about the adventures of Goha.

THE TWO-STOREY HOUSE

One day, Goha decided to build a new house. He had wanted a new house for a long time and he knew the kind of house he wanted. He wanted a house with two storeys – a ground floor and an upper floor.

He did not need the second storey. But he felt that a house with only one storey was not a real house. It would be incomplete. He wanted to be able to look up at a large two-storey building, and say to himself, 'That is my house.'

However, his wife knew that two storeys was much more work. There would be twice as many rooms and stairs and passages to keep clean.

It would also cost a lot of money. His wife could not understand why Goha wanted a two-storey house. Why build a storey they did not need, and which would not be used? Why spend the extra money?

So Goha thought and thought and in the end he made a decision. He decided that he would build two storeys, but he would sell the upper floor, and live on the ground floor. The house would be complete, a real house of two storeys. But he would not have to pay for the second storey and his wife would not have to clean empty rooms.

As the house was in a good district, Goha easily found a buyer. He sold the upper floor to a merchant.

The merchant was very glad, because he also knew the kind of house he wanted.

The merchant had always wanted to live high up, above everybody else. He liked the idea of other people living under him.

So the merchant lived on the upper floor and Goha lived on

5

the ground floor. Each one had got what he wanted and they both lived happily in the house for many years.

But after some years, Goha found that his house was no longer convenient. It was a long way from the court. And the Caliph wanted to see Goha every day. Goha began to dream of a house that would be close to the palace.

He decided to build another house in the part of Baghdad near the palace. But first he wanted to sell his ground floor. And he wanted to do this quickly.

There is no sale without a buyer and who would buy his ground floor? For a quick sale, Goha must sell the ground floor to the merchant.

So Goha thought about the problem. He knew that he had to persuade the merchant to buy the whole house.

While he was at home eating a meal with his wife, he decided what he would do. And the next day he visited the merchant.

He went upstairs and the merchant offered Goha coffee and they spoke of different things. They spoke of the weather and of the rise in food prices.

At last, Goha told the merchant that he had decided to live in another part of the city.

'Well, what are you going to do about the house here?' asked the merchant.

'I don't really know,' said Goha. 'I suppose I'll have to sell my ground floor.'

'Well, I don't want to buy it. I am quite happy upstairs,' replied the merchant.

'Then,' said Goha, 'I will have to find someone else to buy it, won't I?'

'Yes, you will,' said the merchant, who looked very pleased.

So Goha went away and waited for a week. Then he again went back and visited the merchant. The merchant offered Goha some coffee and again they talked of many things. They talked of the weather and of the price of food. Then they talked about their various illnesses.

'Oh, by the way,' said Goha, 'about the house . . .'

'Yes?' said the merchant.

'I found no one to buy the ground floor,' said Goha.

'Then,' said the merchant happily, 'you will have to leave the ground floor empty.'

'Don't you want to buy the ground floor?' asked Goha. Goha tried not to show that he was worried about the house.

'Oh no. I am quite happy here on the upper floor,' said the merchant. 'I like to live above everyone else.'

'You are quite sure?' asked Goha.

'Quite sure,' said the merchant with a smile. He was looking more pleased than ever.

They began to talk of other things, and the day passed pleasantly.

Very early on Saturday morning, the merchant was very surprised to see Goha arrive at the house with twelve workmen. The workmen had come with large hammers and spades.

'Oh,' said the merchant, 'what are you going to do?'

'Well,' said Goha calmly, 'you did not want to buy the ground floor of my house, so I am going to pull it down.'

'Pull it down!' said the merchant. He had gone quite pale and he was no longer looking at all happy. In fact, he could not believe what Goha was saying.

'It's quite simple,' said Goha. 'Let me explain. I don't want my ground floor. I will not use it any more. As I told you, I am going to live in another part of the city and so I will pull down my ground floor.'

The merchant began to shake. He did not know what to say. So he said nothing.

'You can keep your upper floor,' Goha went on, 'but you must remember that there will be no ground floor.'

'No ground floor?' said the merchant.

'You did not want to buy the ground floor of my house,
so I am going to pull it down.'

'No ground floor,' said Goha. 'When the ground floor has gone, don't ask where it is because I am telling you now. These workmen will pull it down.'

And all the workmen smiled at the merchant. From the way they smiled, the merchant could see how much they wanted to pull down the ground floor.

The merchant realised that he could not have an upper floor alone. The upper floor needed to stand on a ground floor.

So the merchant agreed. He bought the ground floor from Goha and he paid the price that Goha asked.

Goha, of course, was very pleased. The Caliph and all the court laughed aloud when Goha told them what had happened.

THE WORLD AFTER DEATH

Goha liked to get away from Baghdad from time to time so that he could be alone.

Life at court was busy and tiring. In the country, he could think clearly. With the sky and the fields and the trees around him, Goha could relax and think about many things.

He would live very simply. Sometimes he would forget to eat. And he did things which might seem strange, or even foolish, to anyone who was watching him.

One day, Goha was sitting in a tree. It was a tall tree, and he sat high up on a branch of this tree, facing the trunk of the tree.

Goha had a saw. He was cutting the branch which he was sitting on with the saw. It was a lovely day. The sun was shining and Goha was singing to himself as he worked.

A man walked along the road. The man was thinking of how far he had to go, and what time he would reach home.

But when the man saw Goha, he stopped and looked up at him. The man's mouth opened to say something. Then his mouth closed again. Finally he spoke.

'Be careful,' the man said, 'you are sitting on the branch. Can't you see? If you cut the branch, you will fall!'

Goha looked down at the man. From the tree, the man looked quite small.

'Will I really fall?' asked Goha with interest.

'Yes, you will certainly fall,' said the man. The man looked proud and pleased with himself. He knew that he was correct.

Goha continued to cut the branch.

It happened suddenly. Goha fell. One moment Goha was up in the tree; the next, he was down on the ground. But he was not hurt. He did not even look surprised.

'Be careful. If you cut the branch, you will fall!'

Goha quickly stood up again and looked at the man. Now they were both on the same level and Goha could see the man properly for the first time.

'You are very clever. You know many things!' said Goha.

The man bowed[1]. He did not deny that he was very clever. In fact, he looked pleased and proud.

'You told me I would fall,' said Goha, 'and I fell. Now tell me something else. Will you answer a simple question?'

The man waited patiently to hear the simple question.

'Tell me,' said Goha, 'when will I die?'

The man looked at Goha. He lifted his hands, and dropped them again.

'I don't know when you will die,' said the man. 'No one can tell you that.'

'You can tell me,' said Goha. He was beginning to enjoy himself.

'But I don't know,' said the man.

'Yes, you do,' said Goha again. 'You are able to see the future. You knew that I would fall from that tree, so you know what will happen.'

Now the man wanted to continue on his journey. He wanted to get away from Goha. So the man thought, and he spoke.

'Listen,' said the man, 'I will tell you. One day, you will be riding on your donkey. Your donkey will slip and nearly fall. In fact, the donkey will slip three times. Then you will die!'

Goha bowed and thanked the man and the man continued on his journey.

Some weeks later, Goha was riding on an old donkey. He was not going anywhere in particular. He was just riding.

Goha liked riding on a donkey because it helped him to think. And now he was deep in thought.

Suddenly the donkey slipped and nearly fell. Then it slipped again. When the donkey slipped a third time, Goha remembered what the stranger had said.

Goha got off the donkey and the donkey walked away slowly. Then Goha knelt down and said his prayers.

Next Goha lay down on the ground. He was wearing a coat, so he pulled the top of his coat over his head. He wanted to look like someone who is dying.

He lay on the ground for a long time.

After a few days, an ambassador[2] from another country passed by. This ambassador was going to the court of the Caliph but he did not know the way to court. All roads in this strange country looked the same to him. When he saw Goha lying on the ground, he stopped. He got down from his horse and spoke to Goha.

'Excuse me,' said the ambassador. 'I am going to the Caliph's palace. Could you tell me the right way?'

Goha did not move. He looked up at the ambassador through the top of his coat. He began to speak in a very low voice, like a voice from the dead.

'When I was alive,' said Goha, 'the road past that baobab tree was the way to the court.'

The ambassador looked at the tree. Then he looked down at Goha, and he looked at the tree again. For a moment he forgot about his journey.

'The tree is still there,' the ambassador said, 'and the road is still there. But what about you? Are you not alive now?'

'No, I am dead,' answered Goha in a quiet voice. Then he was silent and lay still on the ground.

The ambassador wondered if everyone in this strange country behaved in this strange way. But he knew that he could not understand. So he got back on his horse and continued along the road that Goha had shown him. When at last the ambassador came to the court, he saw the Caliph.

After the ambassador had given some important papers to the Caliph, the Caliph offered him some food and drink. While they sat under the leaves of a great palm tree, the Caliph asked the ambassador if he had had an interesting journey.

'Oh yes, most interesting,' replied the ambassador, 'but also a little strange.'

'Strange? Why was it strange?' asked the Caliph.

'Well,' the ambassador explained, 'I met a dead man on the road.'

'A dead man. . . . Is that interesting – or strange?' asked the Caliph.

'Yes,' answered the ambassador, 'he was a most unusual dead man. I did not know the way, and this dead man told me.'

The Caliph seemed very thoughtful. 'Indeed,' he said, 'it is not every day that a dead man speaks to you.'

The Caliph had known Goha for a long time. And when he heard about the 'dead' man, the Caliph started to smile. He guessed that the dead man was Goha because Goha often played tricks. This time he was pretending to be dead. That was Goha's new trick.

The Caliph started to talk to the ambassador about other things. About their two countries, about peace and friendship.

While he was talking, the Caliph was also thinking about Goha. He was thinking how he could wake Goha up from this 'sleep of death'.

There was a man who played the trumpet for the Caliph and his court. He was the royal trumpeter.

After the ambassador had left the palace, the Caliph called the royal trumpeter and told him where to go and what to do. Then the trumpeter immediately left the palace.

The trumpeter soon found Goha who was still lying on the ground. He stood over Goha and blew his trumpet three times.

'Why do you disturb me?' demanded Goha angrily. 'When a man is dead, he wants to be left in peace. So why do you disturb my peaceful death?'

'This is no ordinary day,' answered the trumpeter. 'This is the day you have been waiting for, the day when dead people come back to life!'

'Is that why you blew your trumpet – to bring me back from the dead?' asked Goha.

'Yes,' the trumpeter replied. 'I blew my trumpet three times to bring you back to life. The Caliph now orders you to come to his court.'

'Praise be to God,' said Goha. Immediately he stood up and went with the trumpeter to the court.

When he arrived, the Caliph asked Goha why he had died.

Goha told him the whole story. He told the Caliph how he had sat on the branch of a tree. How a man had told him he would fall. How he had fallen, and the man had said, '. . . the donkey will slip three times. Then you will die!'

'That man thought he was clever,' said the Caliph, 'but he has brought you a lot of trouble.'

'Oh no,' said Goha. 'The man helped me. Because of him, I know now what the world after death looks like.'

The Caliph was interested to hear Goha's story. 'Well,' he said, 'tell me. What could you see in the next world, the world after death?'

'Nothing,' replied Goha. 'There is nothing to see. Nothing at all. To tell the truth. . .' Goha suddenly stopped talking. He was not sure if he should continue with his story.

'Continue,' said the Caliph.

'To tell the truth,' Goha went on, 'I only had one feeling in the next world.'

'What feeling?' asked the Caliph.

'Hunger,' replied Goha with a deep sigh. 'I felt hungry,' he repeated. 'You see, I had no food for many days.'

The Caliph smiled. He immediately understood that Goha was still very hungry, so he told his servants to bring a large meal for Goha.

GOHA AND THE TWO THIEVES

1

A Stolen Sheep

It was Goha's birthday and his wife wanted to prepare a special meal for their friends. She wanted everyone to celebrate Goha's birthday. So she asked Goha to go to market and buy a sheep.

She thought a sheep would make a good meal because she knew that her guests were always hungry. She was looking forward to preparing this meal.

All she needed was the sheep, so she waited patiently for Goha to return from the market.

But Goha returned without the sheep! Instead he had several bruises on his face.

'What's the matter?' asked his wife. 'Didn't you go to the market?'

'Yes, my dear, I went to the market,' replied Goha calmly.

'So you went to the market,' his wife said. 'Good, and where is the sheep?'

Goha looked down at the ground and did not reply.

'Where is the sheep?' asked his wife again. Her voice was louder and she was becoming impatient.

Then Goha looked up and began to tell his story.

'I bought the sheep,' he said quietly.

'Oh, good,' replied his wife. 'You bought the sheep. I did not think you would go to the market for a sheep, and not buy the sheep. But where is it now?'

'Stolen,' said Goha.

'What? Stolen?' his wife asked angrily. 'The sheep was stolen? How? Where?'

'I was on the way home with the sheep,' Goha said. 'You know that road near the well with thick bushes on each side?'

'Yes, I know that road,' said his wife. 'I am always afraid to walk there.'

'Well,' continued Goha, 'I was passing with the sheep, when suddenly a thief jumped out from the bushes. He had a stick and he started to beat me.'

Goha's wife began to shake. She felt afraid for her husband.

'I tried to defend myself,' continued Goha, but the thief was young and strong. I was not thinking about the sheep, because of the blows from the man's stick.'

'My poor husband! Then what happened?' asked his wife who was still shaking.

'While he was beating me, another thief came out of the bushes,' said Goha.

'Another thief!' cried his wife. 'Two thieves in one day! Did the second thief attack you also?'

'Oh no,' explained Goha. 'The first thief only attacked me so I would not see what the second thief was doing.'

'And what was the second thief doing?' she asked.

'Stealing my sheep,' said Goha, lifting his shoulders and spreading his hands. 'When I looked round, the second thief had disappeared with the sheep. Then the first thief ran away also.'

'What did you do then?' asked his wife.

'I came here,' said Goha simply.

'And what are you going to do now?' said his wife.

'I don't know yet,' replied Goha. 'I want to think of a plan.'

Then he sat silently and thought of a plan to trick the two thieves.

'While he was beating me, another thief came out of
the bushes.'

2

A Tree of Gold

Goha called together several men. He armed them with swords, and told them to be his guards.

He led them to the road with bushes on each side, where the two thieves had appeared.

Beyond the bushes there was a forest, and in the forest there was a baobab tree. From the branches of the tree hung fruits, and each of these fruits formed a shell.

Goha went straight to the tree and stood there, looking up at these fruit-shells.

He was thinking as he looked at them, and slowly a smile appeared on his face. The guards waited patiently.

The lowest branch of the tree was close to the ground, so Goha was able to climb up to the branch quite easily. Sitting on the branch he put out his hands, and reached one of the fruit-shells.

Then he took a knife from his pocket and cut a small hole in the shell. From his other pocket he took some gold coins and put them in the hole that he had made. When the gold coins were carefully placed inside the shell, he covered the hole with leaves.

He was careful to leave the fruit hanging from the tree. The fruit was now filled with gold, but it looked just like any other fruit.

Goha came down from the tree and looked at what he had done. The fruit looked as if it had not been touched. It did not look different from the other fruits.

Then Goha climbed the tree again and filled several other fruit-shells with gold. Again he left them hanging from the tree. They also looked as if they had never been touched.

Then he climbed down and looked at the whole tree,

Then he took a knife from his pocket and cut a small hole in the shell.

with all its golden fruit. He smiled again. He was satisfied.

He placed his guards round the tree. They all stood round the precious tree with their swords in their hands.

By now it was night and Goha was ready to sleep. Or at least, Goha was ready to pretend to sleep.

His bed was placed under the tree. And there he lay down, on the bed under the tree, in the middle of the forest.

It was a strange sight, to see Goha in bed under that tree in the moonlight. He was surrounded by his guards with their swords.

All was quiet, except for the sound of Goha snoring[3], or at least, the sound of Goha pretending to snore. The moon continued to shine brightly.

After about an hour, there was the sound of branches being broken, and the sound of feet moving through the bushes.

Goha hid himself under the covers of his bed. Through the trees came the two thieves. They saw the bed and they saw the guards with their swords. The thieves looked at each other curiously. Slowly and carefully they moved towards the tree.

Goha's head could just be seen above the covers at the end of the bed.

One of the thieves walked around looking closely into the face of each of the guards. But the guards continued to stare at the tree. Goha had told them not to move.

The other thief lifted the covers away from Goha's head.

'Wake up, old man,' said the thief.

Goha stopped snoring. Then he opened one eye. He looked at the thief and the thief looked at him. Then the thief looked at the other thief and both thieves looked at the guards. The guards continued to look straight ahead at the tree.

'Are you awake, old man?' asked one of the thieves.

'Yes, I am awake,' said Goha, opening both eyes.

'What are you doing here?' asked the thief. 'Why are you sleeping under this baobab tree?'

'As you asked me, I will tell you,' said Goha. 'I am guarding my gold tree.'

The thief looked at Goha in amazement. He did not know what to say. Now he was more curious than ever.

'What are you guarding?' asked the thief.

'My gold tree,' repeated Goha.

'Which gold tree?' demanded the thief in great surprise.

Goha pointed upwards. 'This gold tree, over my head,' he said. 'This tree is full of golden fruit.'

'Golden fruit?' asked the thief, feeling very excited. 'Why are you guarding it? Is it yours?'

'If the tree were not mine, why would I guard it?' asked Goha simply.

The thief was still not satisfied with Goha's answer. 'How is it yours?' he asked.

'It is mine because I was given it,' Goha explained. Then he added with a smile, 'My father gave it to me.'

The two thieves stood there on each side of the bed, looking down at Goha, and up at the golden fruit, and down again at Goha. Then they looked at the guards who were staring fiercely with their hands on their swords.

'Sell the tree to us,' said the thieves.

'I can't sell the tree,' said Goha as he pulled the covers over his head. 'It belongs to my family, and they want to keep it.'

The thieves went away and wondered what they could do. They were determined to get the tree with its golden fruit, but they could not think how to get it.

Finally one of the thieves spoke. 'Every man has his price. The old man will be glad to sell, if we offer him a big price.'

So they collected one hundred cows and when all the cows were ready, they went back to Goha in the forest.

'Sell us this tree for a big price,' they said.

'What is a big price?' asked Goha.

'We will buy this tree for one hundred cows,' said the thieves.

'One hundred cows,' said Goha, as if he was talking to himself. 'One hundred cows,' he repeated, as if the very sound of the words gave him pleasure.

'But before we give you the hundred cows,' said the thieves, 'you must first prove to us that the fruits of the tree really are full of gold.'

'You do not believe me?' asked Goha.

'Prove it to us,' demanded the thieves. 'Show us the gold from the tree.'

Goha agreed to show them a golden fruit. He told one of the guards to climb up the tree, and cut down some fruit. 'Cut the fruit from the lowest branch,' he said.

The guard climbed up and cut the fruit and gave it to the thieves. The thieves cut open the fruit with their knives. There, inside the fruit, they found gold. Lovely, bright golden coins.

3

The Thieves are Tricked

So the thieves bought the tree, and Goha and his guards took the cows back to his country house. He was very pleased to have one hundred cows.

The thieves were happy also. Every day they came to look at their tree, and every day the fruit ripened a little more. They waited patiently for all the gold that was growing in the fruit of the tree. They dreamt of nothing else.

Finally the fruit was ripe and ready to pick. The thieves came with a big barrel and with big knives, and they cut down all the fruit from the tree.

They were excited at the thought of gold so they opened one of the fruits immediately.

And they found . . . nothing!

They opened another fruit, and another, and another. But there was not a single gold coin in any of the fruit.

They were so angry that they could not speak.

All their lives they had tricked other people. Now they themselves had been tricked! They decided to go at once to Goha and demand that he return their cows.

4

The Thieves Visit Goha

But Goha was ready for the thieves. In fact, he knew when they would come.

Because of his great knowledge, Goha could read the stars. He read in the stars how angry the thieves were and that they were coming to find him.

So, several days before they came, he made a plan.

He went into the forest, and there he caught two gazelles[4]. These two gazelles looked exactly alike. Next, he killed an ox[5] and filled the bladder[6] of the ox with blood.

Then he said to his wife, 'Here is a piece of metal. You must wear it like this.' Then Goha showed his wife how to wear the piece of metal.

'I see,' said his wife, 'I wear it the way soldiers do to protect their chest when they go into battle; it is what they call a breastplate.'

'You are right,' said Goha, 'it is a breastplate.'

And his wife stood in front of the mirror, looking at herself wearing the breastplate.

She smiled. She was pleased with herself. She thought that she looked very handsome. But she did not yet know what else she would have to wear.

Goha now gave her the bladder of the ox, filled with blood.

'Hang this bladder in front of the breastplate, and then put on your dress over everything,' he told her.

His wife put on the bladder filled with blood, and then she put on her dress.

Now she had on all three; the breastplate, then the bladder, and finally the dress. She no longer wanted to look at herself in the mirror. She was afraid that she would now look very ugly.

But Goha was satisfied. 'The thieves will not guess,' he said. 'They will think that is how you always look.

'Now,' said Goha, 'when the two thieves arrive, tell them I am in the fields. They will come to the fields to find me. When they have gone to the fields you will cook the ox and prepare a good meal.'

After he had spoken to his wife, Goha went and locked up one of the two gazelles in a wooden shed. Then he took the other gazelle with him, and went into the fields.

There he waited. He knew from the stars that the thieves would come soon.

When the two thieves found Goha in the fields they talked to him angrily.

'The tree wasn't a gold tree,' they said, 'and in the fruit there were no gold coins.'

Goha nodded at them.

'Give us back our cows,' shouted the thieves.

'All right, all right,' said Goha quietly. 'But have patience. First let's go to my house.'

'Why should we go to your house?' asked the thieves angrily.

'Only because I invite you to a good meal,' explained Goha.

The thieves looked at each other. Then they nodded at Goha. They were happy to accept a meal. Then Goha turned to his gazelle. He said to the gazelle, 'You, gazelle, you are my messenger: go and tell my wife that I am bringing guests. Tell her to cook a good meal for us.'

Then Goha took his hand away from the gazelle and the gazelle ran away. No one ever saw it again. But the thieves thought that the gazelle had gone to Goha's home and given Goha's message to his wife.

The three men left the fields and came to Goha's house. When they reached the house, Goha's wife was waiting to welcome them.

'Dinner is ready,' she said with a smile.

They all sat down at the table and began to eat. Suddenly Goha jumped up from his seat.

'What kind of food is this?' he said. He pretended to be very angry.

Goha's wife jumped up also. She was not pretending. She was really angry. She had spent a long time preparing the meal and she knew that it was a good meal.

'These men are my friends,' cried Goha, pointing to the two thieves. 'They are important people. I am delighted to have them in my house.'

He banged the table with his hand. 'This food is not good enough for them!' he shouted to his wife.

'Not good enough for them!' his wife repeated. 'How can you say that? It is good enough for anyone. It is good enough for the Caliph himself!'

Goha's wife was very angry. Her husband had made her wear the breastplate and the ox bladder under her dress. And now Goha was being rude about her meal in front of strangers.

Of course, Goha knew that his wife would be angry. He wanted her to be angry. He wanted the thieves to think that Goha and his wife were having a terrible argument. So Goha shouted back at his wife as if he was even more angry than her.

'How dare you cook such bad food. How dare you talk to me in such a way,' he shouted. 'I will teach you to be polite to your husband.'

Goha had a knife in his belt. He took the knife and attacked his wife. But he was very careful.

The thieves thought that Goha had pushed the knife into his wife's breast. But really he pushed the knife into the ox bladder that she wore under her dress.

He could not hurt her, because behind the bladder she wore the breastplate.

So when Goha pushed the knife into her breast, blood poured out of the ox bladder. His wife fell flat on the floor.

The thieves stared and said nothing. They thought that Goha had killed his wife.

'I didn't mean to kill her,' said Goha. 'I became very angry. But now I am calm again.'

Then Goha went to a cupboard and took out a stick. It was just an ordinary stick that he used for walking. Goha touched his wife's breast with the stick.

Then he said some strange words that the thieves could not understand.

Then Goha said to his wife, 'Woman, rise again from the floor, rise again from the dead. I forgive you. Rise.'

And Goha's wife rose. She stood up, and she looked quite normal. She looked as if she had never been hurt.

The two thieves looked at her and they looked at each other. They had never seen anyone rise from the dead before.

'Listen,' they said to Goha. 'We want to buy that clever gazelle which took your message to your wife. And your stick, the stick that wakes up the dead – we want to buy the stick also.'

'Well,' said Goha, as if he was surprised. 'I don't know.'

'We will give you one hundred gold coins for the stick and the gazelle,' said the thieves excitedly.

'One hundred gold coins,' repeated Goha. 'Very well, I accept.'

So the thieves gave Goha one hundred gold coins and Goha gave the thieves the stick. The thieves thought that it was a magic[7] stick.

Goha also gave the thieves the other gazelle which he had locked up in the wooden shed. And the thieves thought that this was the gazelle they had seen in the fields.

Then Goha took the hundred gold coins and the thieves went away with the stick and the gazelle.

5

The Thieves Quarrel

At first the thieves were delighted. They were glad to have the 'magic' stick, and they were glad to have the clever gazelle. But as they walked along, they started to argue.

They argued because they had a problem. They were two, but there was only one stick and only one gazelle.

Who should have which?

As they argued, they became very angry. One of the thieves had a big knife in his belt. He got so angry that he pushed his knife into the other thief's breast.

The other thief was not wearing a breastplate, and he was not wearing a bladder. The knife went into his breast. Real blood poured from the wound. He fell dead on the ground. Really dead.

The murderer stood there with the knife in his hand, looking down at his dead friend. He was sad because he had not meant to kill him. Now he was no longer angry.

Then he remembered the 'magic' stick.

He took the stick, and touched the dead body. But a dead man is a dead man. When he touched the body with the stick, the body continued to lie there.

Then the murderer remembered that Goha had spoken some magic words as well. But what were the words?

He did not know. He decided to go back to Goha. He decided to ask Goha to teach him the magic words.

And Goha was expecting him.

Goha knew what would happen. He knew that the two thieves would fight. So he expected one of them to return. Goha called the police to his house. He told them to hide in the next room so they could hear what the thief said.

The thief arrived. He told Goha what had happened. He told Goha how he had killed his friend. He said that he had paid for the stick, and the magic words were part of the stick.

'Without the magic words, the stick is useless,' said the thief. 'The words and the stick go together. I paid for the stick, so tell me the words also. I want to wake my friend from the dead.'

Goha coughed loudly. This was the signal for the policemen to come out of hiding.

'I will give you some words,' said Goha, 'but first these gentlemen will take you away. They have heard your story. You have killed someone and you will be hanged.'

The policemen took the thief away. As he left, the thief turned to Goha.

'What are the words you have for me?' he asked Goha.

Goha looked at the thief for a minute. Then he spoke.

'To hurt a stupid man is wicked,' said Goha. 'But to hurt a clever man is stupid. Never hurt a clever man.'

Then the thief remembered how he and his friend had beaten Goha, and how they had stolen his sheep.

The thief had time to think about Goha's words, before he was hanged for murder. He never did hurt a clever man again.

GOHA BUYS A DONKEY

1

The Greedy Doorkeeper

One day, Goha wanted to buy a donkey. But he had no money to buy it. So he decided to go and ask the Caliph to help him.

When he arrived at the palace, Goha went to see the Caliph. At the Caliph's door stood the doorkeeper.

Usually, the doorkeeper let the members of the court enter without difficulty. But for a long time, the doorkeeper had been jealous of Goha. He was jealous, because Goha had received so many favours[8] from the Caliph. And each favour the Caliph gave to Goha, increased the jealousy of the doorkeeper.

So when Goha came to the Caliph's door, the doorkeeper did not let him enter.

The doorkeeper did not know that Goha wanted a donkey. But the doorkeeper knew that Goha had come to ask the Caliph for a favour.

'You are the Caliph's favourite[9],' said the doorkeeper, 'and I am only his doorkeeper.'

'You are not only his doorkeeper,' Goha told him, 'you are his favourite doorkeeper.'

But the doorkeeper was not satisfied.

'You have all his favours,' he said, 'and I have none.'

'Do not envy me,' said Goha. 'Envy is bad for you. And envy will not make you a favourite poet.'

'I don't want to be a poet,' said the doorkeeper. He was a tall man. He stood up very straight and looked down at Goha.

'I am happy and proud to be a doorkeeper,' he said. 'But I want a share of your good fortune.'

'A share of my good fortune? What do you mean?' asked Goha.

'Whatever favour you get from the Caliph,' the doorkeeper explained, 'you will share with me. You must promise me half of what the Caliph gives you.'

'Whatever I get . . .' repeated Goha thoughtfully.

'And I want you to write down your promise,' said the doorkeeper.

'Yes,' agreed Goha. He was smiling, with a secret smile. But the doorkeeper did not notice. He was in a hurry.

Goha began to write down his promise. 'Whatever I get from the Caliph I will share with you,' he wrote. Then he signed his name underneath.

'Is that what you want?' asked Goha, showing his promise to the doorkeeper.

'Certainly,' said the doorkeeper, 'that is just what I want.'

'You are quite sure?' asked Goha.

'Quite sure,' said the doorkeeper. And he signed the paper also.

Then Goha entered the Caliph's rooms.

Usually, when Goha entered, he bowed to the Caliph with respect. After all, the Caliph had great power.

But this time, when Goha went in, he did not bow to the Caliph. He showed no respect to his ruler. The Caliph was surprised and he spoke to Goha angrily.

'What do you want?' he asked. 'I am busy. Why do you disturb me?'

Goha did not look at the Caliph. Instead, he stared at the wall.

'What do you want?' repeated the Caliph.

'I want you to beat me with a stick,' Goha answered.

'What?' demanded the Caliph. He was so surprised that he could not believe what he heard. 'What did you say?'

'I want you to beat me with a stick,' said Goha. 'I want you to beat me one hundred times.'

The Caliph was very surprised. Although he was angry he still liked Goha and he did not want to beat him.

But since Goha insisted, the Caliph did beat him. But he beat him so gently that Goha could hardly feel any pain.

After Goha had been beaten fifty times, he asked the Caliph to stop.

'Excuse me, I need a rest,' Goha explained.

So the Caliph stopped beating Goha.

Then Goha showed the Caliph the promise that he had signed with the doorkeeper.

The Caliph read the promise. He looked at Goha. He read it again. Now the Caliph was really angry, but he was not angry with Goha. He was angry with the doorkeeper.

'Guards!' called the Caliph loudly.

The guards came running in.

'Bring the doorkeeper here,' he ordered them in a terrible voice.

The guards brought the doorkeeper into the Caliph's room.

'Did you make a promise with Goha?' asked the Caliph.

'Yes,' replied the doorkeeper, smiling. 'Goha promised to share with me everything that you gave him.'

'Well,' said the Caliph, with a loud laugh. 'I have just beaten Goha fifty times with this stick. Now you can have your share.

'Guards,' shouted the Caliph in a loud, angry voice. 'Take this man away and beat him fifty times as hard as you can.'

The guards took the unhappy doorkeeper from the room and led him away to be beaten. He knew now how dangerous it was to trick a clever man, who was also the Caliph's favourite.

2

Goha's Neighbour

After the guards had left with the doorkeeper, the Caliph looked at Goha.

Now the Caliph was calm again. He smiled. He was glad to show his friendship again to Goha.

'Why did you come to see me?' the Caliph asked. He knew that Goha wanted something.

'I need a donkey,' replied Goha.

The Caliph nodded.

'It is normal. Every man should have donkey.'

'Will you give me money to buy the donkey?' asked Goha.

'I will,' said the Caliph. 'I will give you the money you need.'

Goha thanked the Caliph and bowed. Then he left the palace and went happily to market. There he found a man who was selling a donkey. The donkey was handsome and white all over. Goha was in love with it.

Goha bought the donkey and rode home on it. He felt very proud. Everyone in the street turned to admire Goha riding past on his beautiful white donkey.

At home, Goha would not leave his donkey. He kept it with him all the time, even at night. The donkey even slept in the same room with Goha.

Everyone knew about Goha's donkey. The people of the district all talked about it. They all agreed what a handsome donkey it was.

One day, Goha's neighbour had to go on a journey. He was going to marry a girl in the next village and he wanted to travel comfortably.

The neighbour knew that he would be very popular if he appeared in the girl's village on Goha's beautiful white donkey.

So the neighbour came to see Goha. He explained about his marriage, and about his journey to the next village. He asked to borrow the donkey for the journey.

Goha listened in silence. He knew that the road to the next village was very rough. He thought the donkey might get hurt.

Most of all, Goha thought about his beautiful donkey away from home for several days. He loved the donkey too much to let it go away.

'Please lend me your donkey,' asked the neighbour again.

Goha looked straight at his neighbour.

'The donkey is not here,' he said in a firm, clear voice.

At that moment, the donkey brayed[10] from the back of the house. The two men heard it clearly.

'Excuse me,' said the neighbour in surprise. 'Wasn't that your donkey?'

Goha stared at his neighbour. He pretended that he had not heard the donkey.

'What do you mean?' asked Goha.

'That sound we heard,' said the neighbour patiently. 'Wasn't it your donkey braying?'

'What a question!' said Goha. 'Didn't I tell you the donkey is not here?'

The neighbour was certain that he had heard Goha's donkey but he did not know what to say.

'Tell me,' continued Goha, 'which do you believe – me, or a donkey?'

'Well, I . . .' said the neighbour, but he was unable to reply.

'Why did you come to see me?' asked Goha.

'I wanted . . .' began the man.

'Did you come for my donkey, or did you come to listen to my donkey braying?' asked Goha.

The neighbour stood silent.

'Listen,' said Goha. 'If you want to hear a donkey braying, you can. I can bray better than ten donkeys. Are you ready?'

And Goha stood there, with his head back and his face lifted up. And he began to bray loudly.

'Hee haa, hee haa, hee haa . . .'

MOTHER AND CHILD

1
A Baby Pan

One day, Goha's beautiful white donkey was thirsty. Goha had been riding on the donkey all morning. As the sun rose in the sky, the day became hotter and hotter.

By midday, the donkey was very thirsty indeed. When they reached the well near Goha's house, the donkey refused to move. It wanted water from the well.

So Goha got down from the donkey and went into the house of his neighbour.

The neighbour was lying down in the shade. He was fanning himself with the leaf of a palm. At his side was a cool glass of water. First he fanned himself with the palm leaf, then he drank from the water. Then again he fanned himself.

Goha watched his neighbour in silence. The fan cooled the neighbour on the outside, and the water cooled him on the inside.

Goha thought of his donkey, outside in the hot sun. He thought of the donkey waiting, patiently, for water.

'Excuse me,' Goha said.

'You are excused,' said his neighbour, continuing to fan and drink, fan and drink . . .

'My donkey is outside,' Goha told him.

'Is it?' said the neighbour, without interest.

'My donkey is thirsty,' said Goha.

'Yes,' said the neighbour, drinking some water. 'It is a thirsty day. But then in summer, all days are thirsty days.'

'I am glad you feel as I do about summer,' said Goha patiently.
'I want to give my donkey some water.'

'The well is outside,' replied the neighbour.

'Yes, I know,' said Goha. 'The donkey knows too. That is why
it is standing there, waiting.'

'A clever donkey,' said the neighbour.

'I cannot give the donkey water from the well,' said Goha.

'Oh? Why not?' asked the neighbour. For the first time he
seemed to be interested in the conversation.

'I cannot give the donkey water, because I do not have a pan
to hold the water,' said Goha.

'Of course,' the neighbour agreed. 'You need a pan to put the
water in.'

'Have you got a pan?' asked Goha, with a friendly smile.

'Certainly,' said the neighbour. At that moment he was
fanning himself with his right hand. With his left hand he pointed
to the pan lying on the table. 'There is a pan,' he said.

'May I borrow the pan?' asked Goha.

'Certainly,' said the neighbour.

As Goha was leaving with the pan, his neighbour called
him back.

'Heat gives birth to[11] thirst, and the pan will give birth to
water,' the neighbour said. He was glad that he was clever enough
to think of these clever words.

'Thank you for such wise words,' said Goha thoughtfully as he
left. 'I will tell them to the donkey.'

After the donkey had drunk enough water, Goha did not
return the pan to his neighbour. Instead he took the pan home
with him.

He used the pan every day. He filled it with water and the
donkey drank from the pan.

Goha remembered the neighbour's words. 'Come on, don-
key,' he said, 'drink from the pan. And let's see who will give birth
to what.'

A week later, there was a knock at Goha's door. It was the neighbour.

'Excuse me,' said the neighbour. 'I thought you had gone away.'

'Did you? Why did you think that?' asked Goha.

'Because you did not return my pan, I was sure you had gone away,' said the neighbour. 'What else could I think?'

'Since you ask me, I will tell you,' said Goha. 'You could have thought that the pan was giving birth.'

'Giving birth!' the neighbour said in surprise. 'What do you mean?' He had completely forgotten his own words.

'Didn't you say that the pan would give birth to water?' asked Goha politely.

The neighbour nodded.

'You were right, and you were wrong,' Goha continued. 'The pan did give birth, but not to water. No, it did not give birth to water.'

The neighbour waited, wondering what Goha was going to say next.

'Here, I will show you,' said Goha. He went inside the kitchen and returned. In his hand was the pan. And in the pan was – another pan! A tiny little pan, inside the bigger pan.

'What is this?' the neighbour asked curiously.

'The pan gave birth,' said Goha. 'If a pan gives birth, it must give birth to another pan. What else would you expect a pan to give birth to?'

The neighbour looked at the big pan and the small pan and was worried. 'The small pan is not mine,' he said at last.

'Not yours?' said Goha. 'Certainly it is yours! As a child belongs to its mother, so the little pan belongs to the big one. The big pan is yours, and the pan gave birth, so the child is yours. Take both pans.'

The neighbour bowed low before Goha.

'My friend, my dear friend,' said the neighbour. 'You are the most honest man I know. I have never known a house where even pans give birth! Praise be to God. Praise be to the house of Goha!'

2

A Pan Dies

The neighbour carried his two pans back to his house.

A little later, Goha needed the pan again. His donkey refused to drink from any other pan.

Goha loved his donkey so much that he did everything it wanted. So when Goha saw that the donkey wanted this particular pan, he went again to his neighbour.

The neighbour received him with a smile and a bow.

'You are most welcome to my house,' said the neighbour. 'Is there anything I can do for you?'

'Yes, there is,' said Goha. 'Can I borrow the pan again?'

'Certainly,' said the neighbour. 'Which pan would you like to borrow? The mother, or the son?'

Goha thought for a moment. 'The mother,' he said.

The neighbour gave Goha the big pan and Goha took it back to his house. A month passed.

The neighbour used his little pan, but he wanted the big one. Every day he hoped that Goha would return the big pan. Every day he waited at his door, hoping Goha would pass by. He thought that if Goha saw him standing at his door, Goha would remember the big pan, and bring it to him.

But Goha did not pass by. Instead the neighbour saw Goha with his donkey in the distance several times. And the neighbour saw the big pan tied to the donkey's saddle.

The neighbour watched and waited and wondered. Each day he thought of his big pan and hoped that Goha would bring it back the next day. But the days passed, and the weeks passed. And still Goha did not return the big pan. By now, the neighbour was becoming angry.

Finally he went to the house of Goha. Goha asked him to sit down and brought him a cool drink.

They agreed that the weather was still very hot, but not perhaps as hot as it had been a month ago.

There was a short silence. Both men drank some water.

'Yes,' said the neighbour, 'it must be over a month since we met last.'

'True,' Goha agreed. 'Over a month.'

The neighbour coughed. 'Your donkey is well?' he asked.

'Oh, very, very well,' said Goha with a happy smile.

'Your donkey is drinking much water, I suppose?' asked the neighbour.

'Very much water,' agreed Goha. Goha spoke in a friendly way but he was careful not to say anything about the pan.

'Excuse me,' said the neighbour finally. His cheeks were red and he looked embarrassed. 'You borrowed a pan from me.'

Goha nodded his head in agreement. 'I did,' he said.

'Well then,' said the neighbour, 'can I have it back?'

'Unfortunately, you can't,' said Goha.

The neighbour jumped up. 'Why not?' he asked.

Goha pretended to look sad. 'Unfortunately, the pan died,' he said.

'What!' said the neighbour. He was very angry. All these weeks he had waited patiently for Goha to return the pan.

'Yes,' Goha repeated quietly, 'the pan died.'

'Impossible!' exclaimed the neighbour. In his excitement he banged the table with his hand. 'I don't believe you. It was a good pan! A strong pan made of solid copper!'

The neighbour became more and more proud of his pan, and more and more angry with Goha.

'Give me my pan, my strong, solid, copper pan!' shouted the neighbour.

'I can't,' said Goha quietly. 'How can I give you a pan that has died?'

'Such strong pans do not die!' shouted the neighbour.

'You are sure?' asked Goha.

'Very sure,' said the neighbour.

'Look,' said Goha, 'do you remember when I told you the pan had given birth?'

'Yes, I remember,' replied the neighbour.

'And you accepted both pans, the mother and the son?' asked Goha.

'Yes,' said the neighbour.

'So you believed that your pan had given birth?' asked Goha.

The neighbour looked curiously at Goha. He began to wonder if Goha was joking.

'I want my pan,' said the neighbour slowly and seriously. 'If you do not give it to me, I will take you to court[12].'

'Very well,' said Goha. 'Let the court decide. If the pan is so important we will ask for a decision from the court.'

The neighbour went away, and both men waited for the day of the trial[13].

———

At the trial, the judge listened carefully to the history of the pan. It seemed a long history for a pan, but the judge's decision was short.

'All things that give birth, also die,' said the judge. 'Just as the pan gave birth, so the pan has died.'

After the judgement each man returned to his home, and Goha kept the big pan.

A NIGHT OF SURPRISES

In a district near Baghdad there lived a rich man, whose name was Saba. Saba lived in a big house. He had many servants, and was married to a beautiful wife.

In the first years of their marriage the wife loved her husband very much. When he came home, she was waiting for him. When he went away, she waited until his return.

But things changed.

The wife no longer looked after Saba. His meals were not ready when he wanted to eat. The house became untidy.

And she no longer waited for her husband. She no longer noticed whether he was home or away. When Saba spoke to her, she did not seem to listen to him.

The rich husband decided to ask Goha for advice, because he knew that Goha was a wise man. He told Goha about his wife. He told how his wife had changed.

Saba had enough money to buy everything he wanted; yet he had a wife who did not care about him.

'Why has my wife changed?' he asked Goha. 'What has happened?'

Goha, the wise poet, could see what had happened. He did not like to say it, but he had to tell the truth.

'Your wife no longer loves you,' said Goha. 'She loves another man.'

The husband was silent. He could not believe that his beautiful wife would love anyone else.

'It is true,' said Goha. 'It is better that you know. Then you can decide what to do.'

The husband still refused to believe what Goha had said. He left Goha, and returned to his house.

But when Saba thought about Goha's words, he realised they

were true. He knew that Goha had told him the truth and so became annoyed.

He asked himself how Goha knew that his wife loved another man. He thought, Goha knows because Goha is the one she loves. Now all his anger was against Goha. So Saba made a plan. I will punish Goha, he decided.

He ordered his servants to prepare a large wooden box which was big enough to put a man in. The box was then taken to Goha.

At the same time, Saba went secretly to Goha's house and hid in one of the rooms.

When the box arrived, Goha looked at it. He did not know what was inside and he was curious, so he opened the lid of the box.

Saba had been hiding in a corner of the room. Now he suddenly appeared, and pushed Goha into the box. Goha was so surprised that he could do nothing. Before Goha knew what was happening, Saba had pushed him into the box and closed the lid.

There was a river near Goha's house. Saba's servants threw the box into the river and Saba thought that that was the end of Goha. Now I have punished him.

But the box did not sink. It stayed on the surface of the water and floated along the river. Then, at the turn of the river, the box hit the bank. The box stayed on the bank away from the water.

Goha's neighbour walked along the bank of the river every evening. He enjoyed the walk when the air was cool. As he walked along, Goha's neighbour saw the box on the bank and he wondered what was inside.

Goha's neighbour took the knife which he always carried and he broke open the lid of the box. Goha jumped out. He was a bit stiff after his journey on the river, but he was not hurt.

Goha saw that it was his neighbour who had found him in the box. He knew that his neighbour was in love with Saba's daughter. So he thought of a trick.

'You see this box?' said Goha.

'Yes,' replied the neighbour. 'Why are you hiding in that box?'

'My servants will carry this box into the room of Saba's daughter,' Goha explained.

'Saba's daughter!' the neighbour said excitedly. He had been dreaming about the rich man's daughter for a long time.

'You see,' whispered Goha, 'the rich man's daughter is waiting for someone to appear in this box.'

The neighbour was so excited that he did not hesitate. 'I have always loved her,' he said. 'I shall appear before her. Yes!'

And the neighbour jumped quickly into the box.

'All right,' said Goha, 'lie down and wait.'

The neighbour lay down in the box and Goha closed the lid and walked away, smiling.

What a strange night, Goha thought. First I am thrown into a box for something I have not done. Then my neighbour jumps into the box for something he wants to do. What a strange night!

THE HOUSE IN THE SKY

1

Saba's Lie

The rich man, Saba, was angry with Goha. He felt that Goha had defeated him.

So Saba thought how he could trick Goha. He wanted to show that he was as clever as Goha.

Because he was rich and powerful, Saba was friendly with the Caliph. The Caliph always listened to what Saba said.

Saba knew that Goha was the Caliph's favourite. He knew that the Caliph protected Goha in the way a father protects a son.

So Saba thought, I will make the Caliph angry with Goha. I will make them enemies. Then Goha will have to leave the country.

Saba knew that the Caliph did not like men who boasted[14]. So Saba decided to tell a lie to make Goha appear boastful.

When Saba went to see the Caliph, the Caliph asked him about his farms and houses. Saba explained how he was building a new summer-house. He asked the Caliph to visit him, as his first guest, at this new summer-house. The Caliph accepted Saba's invitation.

They spoke together of the problems of building a house.

'It takes a long time to build a house,' said Saba.

'That is natural,' said the Caliph. 'A house is not built in a day.'

'No,' Saba agreed, 'a house is not built in a day. But Goha told me that he can build a house in three days.'

'In three days!' exclaimed the Caliph laughing. 'That is impossible.'

'True,' said Saba.

'What kind of house can Goha build in three days?' asked the Caliph. He was already getting angry that Goha should boast like this.

'Not just an ordinary house,' said Saba. 'Goha says that he can build a house in the sky in three days.'

'A house in the sky!' exclaimed the Caliph. He stood up. Saba stood up also.

'Send Goha to me!' shouted the angry Caliph.

Saba bowed, and went away.

Of course Saba had lied to the Caliph. Goha had not said that he could build a house in the sky, but the Caliph believed Saba's story.

––––––

When Goha was brought to the Caliph, he did not know why the Caliph was angry. The Caliph had always protected him. The Caliph had been like a father to Goha.

And so Goha did not argue with the Caliph. He did not even ask himself why the Caliph was angry.

'I have a job for you,' said the Caliph. He spoke in an angry voice. 'You will begin immediately.'

'Certainly,' said Goha. 'May I ask what job you wish me to do?'

'I want you to build a house,' said the Caliph.

'It will be a pleasure,' said Goha with a polite bow.

The Caliph smiled, but his smile was not friendly. 'This is no ordinary house,' he said.

Goha waited.

'Since you are so clever . . .'

Goha bowed again as the Caliph spoke.

'. . . you will build this house in the sky,' said the Caliph.

Goha stood there, unable to say anything. He could not believe the Caliph's words.

'That is all,' said the Caliph, waving his hand.

Goha turned to go.

'Oh, one more thing,' said the Caliph. 'You will build this house in three days.'

'I will do as you say,' said Goha.

'And don't forget,' said the Caliph. 'If you have not built this house in the sky at the end of three days, you will leave the country. You will go and live in some other country.'

Goha said nothing. He bowed, and went away, deep in thought. He loved his country, and he did not want to leave it. And yet – how could he build a house in the sky?

2

Goha Waits for the Wind

Goha began to think about what he would do. And then he walked out of the town.

Outside the town where Goha lived, there was a field of bamboo. These bamboo sticks grew very strong, and very tall.

The field was separated from the town by a small river. It was very quiet, and nobody came there. So Goha could work in secret, without anyone seeing what he did.

Goha cut down many sticks of this bamboo and he cut them to different sizes.

As he worked, he often looked at a drawing he had made. On this drawing he had written the size of each piece of bamboo.

When all the sticks were ready, he laid them out on the ground, one beside the other.

Then he took a roll of paper that he had brought with him to the field. The paper was very thin, yet strong. Goha cut the paper into an unusual shape.

Then Goha fitted the paper carefully round the sticks. He knew exactly the position of each stick because it was marked on the drawing.

When it was ready, he looked at it. He turned it over, this way and that. The sticks of bamboo were very light, and the paper was thin. Goha had made something that was both light and strong. Goha had made a kite. The kite was ready to fly, ready to float in the air.

But this was no ordinary kite. From a distance, the kite looked just like a house. A house without a roof. Then Goha tied small bells to the four corners of the kite.

The kite had the shape of a house, but Goha still had not finished. He painted doors and windows on the paper. He used bright colours, and the house looked very gay. And then he painted little men onto the paper. From a distance, it looked as though these little men were working on the house.

Goha had also brought a long thread of strong cotton with him. When the kite was finished, he tied one end of the cotton to the kite, and he tied the other end to a tree. Then he waited.

He had done all that a man can do, even a clever man. He had made the kite but he could not make it fly. Only the wind could make the kite fly. Without the wind, the kite lay on the ground.

Soon it began to get dark. Goha lay on his back, watching the stars appearing in the sky.

God will help me, said Goha to himself. God will provide wind.

He painted doors and windows on the paper. And then he painted little men onto the paper.

Then Goha turned over and fell asleep.

———

While Goha was sleeping, he had a dream.

He dreamt of a great palace, high in the sky. The palace was above the clouds where the sky was always blue.

In his dream, Goha stood at the door of the palace, waiting to enter. Other people came and went freely, but Goha could not go in.

Finally a messenger came out of the palace and spoke to Goha. 'You have come too soon,' said the messenger.

'When shall I come?' asked Goha. 'When is my time?'

'Only God can tell you that,' said the messenger. 'But God is not here.'

'Where is God?' asked Goha.

The messenger looked down through the clouds. He seemed to see everything that went on below.

'God is everywhere,' he said, 'but most of all He is busy on earth.'

'What is He doing, on earth?' asked Goha.

'He is saving men from their own foolishness,' answered the messenger.

'Do men have no goodness then?' asked Goha.

'Yes, sometimes,' said the messenger. 'Their goodness is uncertain, like the wind. But God waits. If the wind does not blow today, it will certainly blow tomorrow.'

———

The next morning when Goha awoke, the sun was already shining brightly. Even before he opened his eyes, he knew that something was different. He knew something important had happened.

He sat up suddenly, listening to the strong wind that seemed to sing through the tall bamboos. And when he looked up, he saw his kite high in the sky.

My prayer is answered, thought Goha. Praised be God!

3

The Caliph Sees the House

Then Goha went to the Caliph, who was still eating his breakfast.

The Caliph did not like to be disturbed at breakfast. In the morning he was always very sleepy.

But Goha knew that this was the right moment for his plan. He asked to see the Caliph immediately.

When the Caliph heard that Goha wanted to see him, he knew that it must be about the house in the sky. The Caliph forgot that he was still sleepy. He finished his breakfast quickly and Goha was brought in.

'Well,' said the Caliph, 'have you built your famous house in the sky?'

Goha did not answer directly. Instead, he asked the Caliph, 'Am I an honest man?'

'You know if you are an honest man or not,' the Caliph answered. 'That is each man's secret.'

'But how can I prove to you that I am honest?' Goha asked.

The Caliph thought for a moment.

'I will only believe something,' he said slowly, 'if I see it with my own eyes.'

'Are you sure?' asked Goha quickly.

'Certainly, I will always believe what I see,' said the Caliph.

Then Goha led the Caliph into the royal garden. Goha

pointed to the sky and the Caliph looked up. And there far away in the sky, the Caliph saw a house.

'What do you see,' asked Goha, 'with your own eyes?'

The Caliph looked again at the house. He was very surprised.

Of course, in those days kites were unknown. The Caliph had never seen a kite before. He had never heard of a kite, which can be kept in position by a steady wind. He did not know that the wind can be used in this way.

But Goha knew. Goha had invented the kite. He had built the kite and made it look like a house – a house in the sky. And the Caliph believed what he saw.

The Caliph continued to stare. He could not stop looking at the house in the sky.

'The roof . . .' said the Caliph in wonder.

'Yes, my men are still busy, as you can see.'

And indeed, the Caliph saw little men in the house. He saw them because Goha had put them there – he had painted them with his paintbrush.

The Caliph also heard the men as they worked, hammering on the roof.

Of course the Caliph only thought that he heard the men working. What he really heard was the sound of the bells that Goha had put on his kite.

'I need some more wood for the roof,' said Goha. 'You can see that the house is very large. It is big enough for a palace.'

Then Goha bowed politely.

The Caliph was finding it more and more difficult to be angry with Goha. Perhaps he even felt a little ashamed.

'I will send you some more wood for the roof,' the Caliph said.

'If you would also send some men . . .' said Goha.

'Why do you need more men?' asked the Caliph in surprise.

'I need men to carry the wood up to the house,' said Goha.

The Caliph looked again at the 'house', sailing high up in the windy sky. He was deep in thought, but then he spoke.

He had built the kite and made it look like a house –
a house in the sky.

'Make sure my men find their way down again,' said the Caliph.

Then he ordered some of his men to go with Goha.

4

The Sky Belongs to God

Goha led the men out of the town to the field of bamboo. When they reached the river, Goha showed them a tree. The cotton that was tied to this tree went all the way up to the kite.

'How do we get to your house in the sky?' asked the men.

'This is the only path to my new house,' said Goha. 'There is no other way.'

The men stood there, holding the heavy wood which the Caliph had given them. They looked at the thin cotton thread, climbing high into the sky. And they looked at the house, as it moved in the wind, high up in the sky.

The men talked about the problem among themselves. They talked seriously about the distance between the tree and the house, and about the weight of the wood.

They had always obeyed the Caliph's orders. But now they could not walk up the thin cotton thread to the house in the sky. So the workmen returned to the palace carrying the wood with them.

'Why have you not finished the roof of my palace in the sky?' the Caliph asked his workmen.

'The palace is in the sky, but we are on earth,' they explained. 'The way to the palace is on a thread of cotton. We are only men. We cannot walk into the sky – not on a thread of cotton.'

'You are right,' said the Caliph. 'No one can walk on a thread into the sky. The sky belongs to God; man walks on the earth.'

At this moment Goha appeared.

'Then,' asked Goha, 'why did you ask me to build a house in the sky? Am *I* not a man?'

The Caliph was silent. He knew that there was no answer.

Points for Understanding

THE TWO-STOREY HOUSE

1 Why did the merchant want to live on the top floor of Goha's house?
2 How did Goha persuade the merchant to buy the ground floor?

THE WORLD AFTER DEATH

1 How did Goha fall from the tree?
2 What did Goha do when his donkey slipped three times?
3 What was the one feeling that Goha had in the next world?

GOHA AND THE TWO THIEVES

1 Why did Goha want to trick the thieves?
2 Why did the thieves want to buy the tree?
3 What did the thieves find when the fruit was ripe?
4 How did Goha know when the thieves would come to his house?
5 Why did Goha's knife not kill his wife?
6 What happened to the two thieves?

GOHA BUYS A DONKEY

1 What promise did Goha make to the doorkeeper?
2 Why did Goha ask the Caliph to beat him?
3 Why did Goha refuse to lend the donkey to his neighbour?
4 Did the neighbour really hear the donkey braying?

MOTHER AND CHILD

1 Why did Goha want to borrow his neighbour's pan?
2 What did Goha say when he gave two pans back to his neighbour?
3 What was the judge's decision about the pan?

A NIGHT OF SURPRISES

1 Why did Saba come to see Goha?
2 Who did Saba think his wife was in love with?
3 What trick did Saba play on Goha?
4 Why did the neighbour jump into the box?

THE HOUSE IN THE SKY

1 What lie did Saba tell the Caliph?
2 What did Goha make with the bamboo and the paper?
3 Why did Goha wait for the wind?
4 What did the Caliph think when he heard the bells on the kite ringing?
5 Why could the workmen not obey the Caliph's orders?

Glossary

1 **bow** (page 12)
  to say hello to a person by bending your head low towards him or her.
2 **ambassador** (page 13)
  a person who visits another country to do business between his or her
  government and the government of that country.
3 **snore** (page 22)
  to make a noise through your nose when you are asleep.
4 **gazelle** (page 25)
  a small animal like a deer.
5 **ox** (page 25)
  a large animal used for pulling carts. Its meat can be eaten.
6 **bladder** (page 25)
  part of an animal's insides. Like a stomach, it can be filled with air or
  water. Goha fills it with blood.
7 **magic** (page 30)
  able to do things in stories which are not possible in real life.
8 **favour** (page 32)
  a gift or help given to a person by someone else.
9 **favourite** (page 32)
  Goha received many favours or gifts from the Caliph because he was
  the Caliph's favourite. This means he was very much liked by the
  Caliph.
10 **bray** (page 36)
  the noise made by a donkey.
11 **give birth to** (page 39)
  to produce something. When a baby is born, its mother gives birth to
  the baby.
12 **take someone to court** (page 44)
  you try to prove to a judge that someone has done you wrong. The
  judge makes a decision in a special building called the court. This is
  not the same as the Caliph's court.
13 **trial** (page 44)
  when a judge listens to people in a court and makes a decision, it is
  called a trial.
14 **boast** (page 48)
  to speak a lot about how important or clever you are.

Shane *by Jack Schaefer*
Old Mali and the Boy *by D. R. Sherman*
Bristol Murder *by Philip Prowse*
Tales of Goha *by Leslie Caplan*
The Smuggler *by Piers Plowright*
The Pearl *by John Steinbeck*
Things Fall Apart *by Chinua Achebe*
The Woman Who Disappeared *by Philip Prowse*
The Moon is Down *by John Steinbeck*
A Town Like Alice *by Nevil Shute*
The Queen of Death *by John Milne*
Walkabout *by James Vance Marshall*
Meet Me in Istanbul *by Richard Chisholm*
The Great Gatsby *by F. Scott Fitzgerald*
The Space Invaders *by Geoffrey Matthews*
My Cousin Rachel *by Daphne du Maurier*
I'm the King of the Castle *by Susan Hill*
Dracula *by Bram Stoker*
The Sign of Four *by Sir Arthur Conan Doyle*
The Speckled Band and Other Stories *by Sir Arthur Conan Doyle*
The Eye of the Tiger *by Wilbur Smith*
The Queen of Spades and Other Stories *by Aleksandr Pushkin*
The Diamond Hunters *by Wilbur Smith*
When Rain Clouds Gather *by Bessie Head*
Banker *by Dick Francis*
No Longer at Ease *by Chinua Achebe*
The Franchise Affair *by Josephine Tey*
The Case of the Lonely Lady *by John Milne*

For further information on the full selection of
Readers at all five levels in the series, please refer
to the Heinemann Guided Readers catalogue.

Heinemann English Language Teaching
A division of Reed Educational and Professional Publishing Limited

**This book is to be returned on or before
the last date stamped below.**

≤ 1 OCT 2004

LIBREX

Caplan

0151 - 291 - 2000

IVERPOOL HOPE UNIVERSITY COLLEGE